THE WOUNDED SPIRIT

BREAKING FREE FROM THE WOUNDS OF YOUR PAST

THE WOUNDED SPIRIT

FOREWORD BY
BISHOP JEFFREY D. HOLLIDAY

Unless otherwise indicated,
all Scripture references are from the
King James Version of the Bible

THE WOUNDED SPIRIT

BREAKING FREE FROM THE WOUNDS OF YOUR PAST

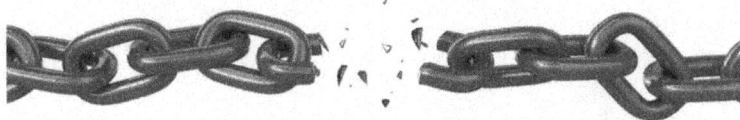

R.R.H. Creation Publications
P.O. Box 800 Monee, IL 60449
reginaholliday@aol.com

DEDICATION

I dedicate this book to my mother, Cora Dillard. The most wonderful woman I've ever known. I am honored to have called you mother. It is with much earnest gratitude I thank you. Thank you for the numerous things you instilled and imparted into my life. As I look back, I recall the words and wisdom you spoke to me and find myself saying, "That's what she meant" quite often. Thank you for the love, knowledge and insight that is being manifested in my life today.

FOREWORD
By Bishop Jeffrey D. Holliday

In the times we live in there are many people, in the world in general and the church specifically, that are suffering in silence from very deep wounds that are going untreated.

I'm excited about our opportunity to face the healing process head on! Through this book I believe that God will challenge, encourage and strengthen you into the newness of life that you so richly deserve.

Be Blessed.

THE WOUNDED SPIRIT

BREAKING FREE FROM THE WOUNDS OF YOUR PAST

Table Of Contents

INTRODUCTION

Life is like a journey and while on this journey we have many different experiences. It's these encounters that give us all a story. We get exposed to many different things on this journey. These things can affect our lives negatively as well as positively. Our life course can change because these events can cause our mindsets to be altered and damage us emotionally.

Many people are struggling and having difficulties now because of where the journey of life has taken them in the past. Some are trapped and paralyzed by their past and unable to move forward.

Holding on to past hurts, pains or offenses will cause you to constantly relive that pain and sometimes cause sickness, anxiety and depression.

There are more people who suffer from depression and anxiety than ever before. According to [1]The National Health Institute of Mental Health, "18.8 million American Adults suffer from clinical depression. That is 9.5% of the entire adult population."

There are more people taking prescription medications today than ever before. These medications are being prescribed to help even out moods and calm emotions to help people get through their day to day life. God created us with emotions. It's when these emotions are unbalanced that people begin looking to other ways of getting back to that state of balance they once knew. Many people are under the false impression that these medications will get rid of these difficult feelings. This is not true. Our emotional state plays a very important role in our ability to function properly in life. These emotions play a vital role in getting us to move or helping us reach a higher level of understanding that enrich our ability to deal with life. Unacknowledged feelings or emotions can cause big problems. It is only when we learn to recognize feelings in the right way that we form a balanced emotional state of well being.

Unacknowledged emotional wounds can lead to inner turmoil. When the wounds of the past go unhealed, it's similar to an infected wound. As a health care professional, when I would assess a wound, my goal was to first create a plan of care to heal the wound. If there was infection in the wound, my plan of care had to go from healing the wound to getting the infection out first, because an infected wound won't heal.

The infections that come to invade a wounded spirit are unforgiveness, bitterness, anger, hatred, being easily offended, resentment and violence, just to name a few.

Maybe you have been wondering why you can't seem to move forward and are always angry. You may have a wounded spirit that's infected. You must first get the infection out before the wound will heal. If you've spent much time dealing with the wounds of your past start dealing with the infections first then proceed to heal the wounds.

As you read this book, it is with heartfelt sincerity that I welcome you to journey with me back through my past. I open parts of my life, to expose the enemy and render him powerless, that you may find restoration, healing and hope in your life.

As we take this journey, I pray you will come to know that God wants to heal you from your past and move you into your God given destiny. Realize that you too have a story, it matters and someone needs to hear it.

THE WOUNDED SPIRIT

BREAKING FREE FROM THE WOUNDS OF YOUR PAST

CHAPTER 1

IN MY MOTHER'S WOMB

My mother was thirty nine years old when she gave birth to me. That may not seem like it's too old to have a child, especially since it isn't uncommon to hear of a woman giving birth in her fifties and sixties today. During this particular time in my mother's life, she was very sick. I was her fourteenth pregnancy and the doctors had already warned her that having another child could cost her her life.

I never asked my mom any questions regarding her pregnancy but if I could speculate using the above information, I'm sure it could not have been easy.

During this very difficult time she carried me for nine months and nourished me. There were many other things happening in my mother's life that would influence the course of my life.

While in my mother's womb, before I knew life on this earth, the spirit of rejection entered my life. The sickness, stress and other difficulties she was going through had a direct affect on me even before I was born.

I believe many things a mother experiences during pregnancy will affect her unborn child physically, emotionally as well as spiritually. An article by [2] EpochTimes states, "A pregnant woman's thoughts have a physical connection to her unborn child." [3] Dr. Thomas Verny, established as one of the world's leading authorities on the effects of prenatal environment on personality development says, "Everything the pregnant mother feels and thinks is communicated through neuro-hormones to her unborn child, just as surely as are alcohol and nicotine." In this same article [4] Dr. Deepak Chopra states, "When a pregnant mother is anxious, stressed, or in a fearful state, the stress hormones released into her bloodstream cross through the placenta to the baby."

[5] Luke 1:41 Says, "And it came to pass, that, when Elisabeth heard the salutation of Mary, the baby leaped in her womb; and Elisabeth was filled with the Holy Ghost." In this scripture, when Elisabeth heard Mary's greeting, the baby leaped in her womb. So we see that what Elisabeth experienced had a direct affect on her unborn child.

In the book [6] Comfort for the Wounded Spirit, Frank and Ida Mae Hammond shared a story someone shared with them regarding a woman who identified herself as the daughter of a 'Leading American Psychologist.' She related that her father has proposed a new approach to abortion. He advised that a woman wanting to abort her child be instructed to verbalize strong words of rejection to the fetus. The woman reported her father as saying that sixty percent of such verbally rejected babies naturally aborted.

An article by [7]ChrisFieldBlog.com says that rejection is "Cutting off the Love Supply". This article goes on to say, "When those who should love and accept us refuse to do so we are hurt on the inside. Rejection is most strongly felt when the person who is (or seems to be) cutting off the love supply is someone we expect to love us."

A spirit of rejection can enter a person in many ways. We see this spirit can enter while still in a mother's womb due to the distress or shock during pregnancy. Also the words or actions of parents, siblings, teachers or other authority figures can open the door for the spirit of rejection. Trauma during pregnancy or at birth is still another way this spirit can enter someone's life.

To reject, according to [8]dictionary.com, means to refuse

Illustration by Ann King

to accept, to discard as useless or unsatisfactory. There are many people who have been made to feel discarded and useless.

Rejection causes a wounded spirit. Almost everyone experiences rejection at one time or another in their life. Many people now realize that hurts from their past still afflict them today, even people in the body of Christ. Rejection may be an unsuspecting culprit in many cases. This stubborn spirit can become a stronghold and affect a person's life in many ways unless healing occurs.

When you are born with a spirit of rejection, if this spirit is not dealt with, a child can grow up with many things dominating their life. The spirit of rejection attacks the very person you are. It distorts your identity and causes you to live in a false reality. Feelings of worthlessness, insecurity and hopelessness are a daily reminder of the self rejection that overwhelms the life of a person rooted in rejection.

The wound of rejection was a daily reality in my life. I struggled for such a long time not knowing why I was the way I was. The Lord began to show me this major hindrance. That's when I realized it would take His power to over come this.

The Lord took me through a process of deliverance. I had to make a conscious effort to reject the spirit of rejection and break my agreement with it. I had to learn what God has said about me and make Godly confessions over my life regularly. God taught me how to love myself, helping me to see myself as valuable and understand the love He has for me. This process was long and sometimes very difficult. Now I've come to realize and understand the real love of God and this has helped me in overcoming the wound of rejection.

The Bible asks a question in ₉Romans 8:35, "Who shall separate us from the love of Christ?" I was determined not to allow rejection to separate me from God's love. I realized God has always been there, especially through the difficult times. I wasn't capable of experiencing His love because of the distorted perception rejection brought in my life.

If you were born with the spirit of rejection, rejected as a child, rejected in a marriage or a friendship, one of the most important things to know is that God loves you. He wants you to experience His love. When you begin to value and appreciate yourself from God's view point it will change your life.

THE WOUND OF SEXUAL ABUSE

When I first thought about writing a book, the Lord told me to think about my first memory of being alive. As I started to think, memories began to flood my mind. The first memory I can recall is when I was two years old. As I continued to move forward in my thinking, I started thinking about something that happened when I was three years old. I spent over forty years of my life with this scene playing over and over in the back of my mind. Every time this thought came up I would tell myself, "It's no big deal". One day the Lord spoke to me and said, "It is a big deal." I didn't realize the thing that I saw as no big deal was causing guilt and shame to dominate my life. I walked around for many years feeling inadequate and with low self esteem. I never understood why until that day. The Lord brought to the front of my mind the fact that I had been sexually violated when I was three years old. It was a big deal and it was time to deal with it.

The age of three is a crucial developmental stage in a child's life. A three year old should be building self

Illustration by Ann King

confidence, self esteem and independence. When this happened to me it hindered my emotional development. My self esteem and self confidence became stalled so I was unable to properly move forward in these areas. Now I understood why after all that time I was still struggling with these issues.

Being introduced to sex at such an early age causes a child to have a distorted view of sex. It can cause promiscuity, perversion, frigidity and many other things to happen.

At three, I wasn't capable of comprehending such a violation. At that time, I didn't know what to feel emotionally. My mind wasn't developed to process this so I pushed it to the back of my mind and continually told myself it wasn't a big deal.

As God began to take me through the healing process, I started to feel a terrible pain in my heart. Every time I would think about what happened to me I would cry. Going through this process, God told me the guilt and shame I carried all these years wasn't mine to carry any longer, it wasn't my fault and I could let it go. As I begin to let these things go, I started to grieve for that three year old child. I spent many days and nights crying and feeling the pain I never allowed to come up.

This is another example of how my past was paralyzing me. I was unable to move forward in my life because I was emotionally wounded. I couldn't pinpoint what the problem was but I knew something wasn't right.

This process of healing is a journey the Lord took me on when I least expected it. Because God is all knowing He knew the exact time to bring this up in my life. It is so important to allow the Lord to journey you to and through any past hurts or pains. Never attempt to navigate through these treacherous territories without being lead by the Holy Spirit. It's the spirit of God that will lead us into all truth. There are some things we may have suppressed because we are not emotionally able to deal with them at this time. It is only with the Holy Spirit's leading and directing should we approach these things so we may be armed and equipped to properly deal with them.

FIFTEEN AND PREGNANT

I can remember having my first boyfriend at nine years old. I didn't understand what that meant but at the time he liked me so I liked him. That's when it began for me. I always had a boyfriend from that point on. By the time I turned fifteen I was pregnant. When I found out I was pregnant I was embarrassed, disappointed, and ashamed. I spent the entire pregnancy worrying about what others would think.

After nine months, I had to quickly learn how to be a mother. I was still dealing with all of those unresolved emotional issues from my past, not to mention the ones I was going through being fifteen and pregnant. This wasn't a happy time for me. All throughout the pregnancy I thought about my future and what I would do. I spent the early months of my pregnancy with severe morning sickness. I couldn't keep anything down and just the smell of certain things would make me nauseated.

Due to this being my first pregnancy, I didn't know what to expect. I was overwhelmed with all the changes that began to occur with my body. I was an emotional wreck and couldn't concentrate in school. I was so pre-occupied with so many things and I didn't have much peace at all.

In an article by [10]eHow.com entitled Effects of Teenage Pregnancy, it states, "Teen pregnancy is always a serious matter. Most teens are unprepared to have a baby and sometimes seek alternatives to having a baby. Teen girls may not be prepared for the physical toll that pregnancy causes on one's body. Many teens that get pregnant become scared and panicked. Confusion about right decisions to make for herself and her child, resentment of the child's father and fear about giving birth may all cause a great deal of stress. This combined with the hormones from her changing body, may result in a very erratic and unhealthy emotional state."

As I look back at that time in my life I know it was only the grace of God that brought me through it. I realize that being wounded took me from one disastrous phase of my life to another. I wasn't capable of making the best decision from the emotional place I was in. Almost every decision I

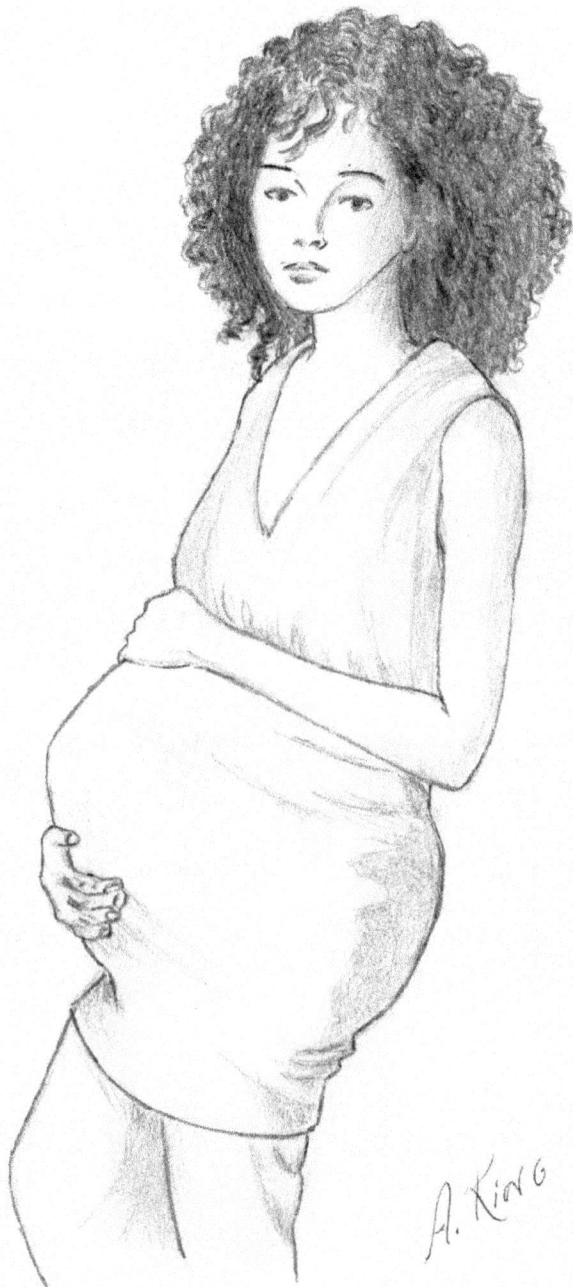

Illustration by Ann King

made was based from a view clouded by pain and hurt.

There are many young girls who are contemplating being sexually active or already are, because of a void they have on the inside. Giving yourself to someone at such a young age, when you are not mature enough to handle where that may take you, can lead you into a more difficult place. God created sex for marriage. When we get outside of the will of God there are always consequences to our actions. These consequences may include unwanted pregnancy, ungodly attachment, and sexually transmitted disease, just to name a few.

Dealing with emotional hurts can help you make better decisions about your life. Don't allow the pain to keep you in a perpetual motion of wrong decisions. These wrong decisions will affect your life for many more years to come.

THE WOUND OF PHYSICAL ABUSE

After I gave birth to my son I was overjoyed at such a beautiful sight. Shortly after his birth the relationship I was in became very strained. Looking back, there were many obvious red flags, but I was too naïve to perceive them. My relationship pictures told me that if you are with someone, you stay with them no matter what. As I grew up, I watched some of the women in my family tolerate abuse. I didn't realize that these relationship pictures were part of an image that had already been ingrained in my mind. At that time, I had no idea I had a choice in this abusive relationship. My mind told me to stand by my man no matter what.

I have many dreadful memories of the years of abuse I endured. I have had a concussion, fractured ribs, black eyes and bruises, just to name a few things. During this time I remember reasoning with myself thinking, "If I fight back maybe I won't get hit again." When that didn't work I decided if I didn't hit back maybe it would stop. Nothing worked! I learned to tolerate many things. If I didn't say the right thing I would get hit. So I started trying to anticipate what this person wanted me to say. I thought he would change and the abuse would stop. That never happened. I left many times only to be lured back by many empty promises and my own co-dependency.

[11]Relationship-tips-for-you.com states "Abusive relationship statistics is an area needing much attention in order for us to get an accurate picture of the reality of the situation. The issue is so hidden, and in spite of any advances that have been made, there is so much that is still not known, because we don't know what goes on behind close doors. Combined with this is the reluctance by many of those who are in abusive relationships, to disclose what is happening to them for various reasons. These reasons are part of the abusive relationship statistics that are not included in the reports we get. They don't disclose, because they are too scared or embarrassed. Other abusive relationship statistics we do know indicate that domestic violence is still the single biggest threat or injury to women, more than; heart attack, cancer, stroke, car accidents, muggings, and rapes com-

bined. Other statistics show that in the United States, three women are killed every day by a husband, boyfriend or cohabitating partner in abusive relationships."

On one of the occasions after being beat, I went to the hospital because I was in a lot of pain. I remember the nurse asking me what happened. After I told her, she asked me if I wanted to make a report. I got scared and told her no. I was treated and released with a slight concussion and a fractured rib.

I understand why parts of the abusive relationship statistics aren't included in the report. I, like many other women, was too afraid to expose the hidden secret of abuse. So many women won't tell. There are so many women who are being abused almost daily behind closed doors still making excuses and giving reasons why they have to stay.

When I did get the courage to get out of this abusive relationship I was even more emotionally damaged and broken. It's been over twenty years since I left and it was one of the best decisions I have ever made in my life.

From the ages of 16 to about 24 or so, I stayed. I stayed in an abusive relationship that tore my self-esteem to shreds;

a relationship that put me in harms way on many occasions, not just because of the abuse but because of the bad decisions I agreed to. This relationship kept me on edge, constantly having to be something that I wasn't to please someone else; a relationship that could have cost me my life.

You may be wondering, "Why did you stay?" Well, as I look back, I believe I stayed because I was looking for love. I stayed because I was trying to fill a void on the inside. I stayed because I thought I was supposed to. I stayed because I didn't love myself and I felt like I was getting what I deserved. I stayed because I didn't know who I was. I stayed because of the history of my life; the history of rejection, the history of low self esteem, the history of guilt and the history of sexual abuse. All these things kept me paralyzed and blinded to the life I deserved. I didn't know how to create boundaries or limitations for people in my life, so I stayed.

Abuse occurs when something or someone is not being used for its intended purpose. Everything was made for a specific purpose. A washing machine was made to wash clothes. A stove was made to cook food. A plastic bag was

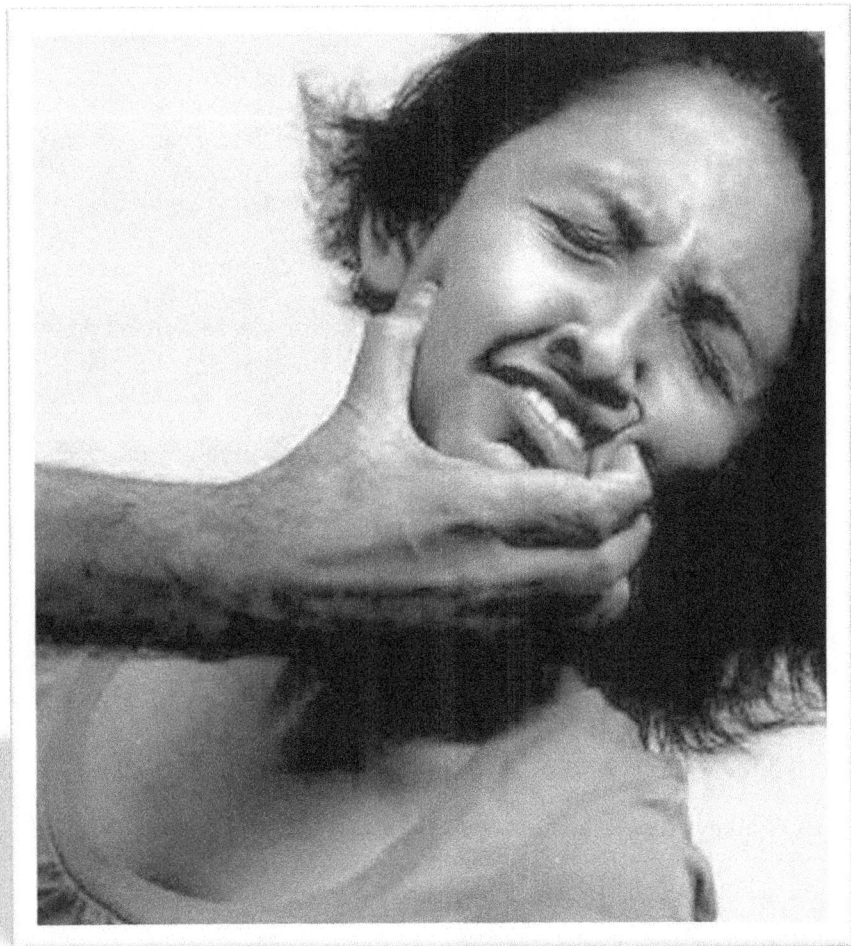

created to hold things in. You were created to be loved, to give love and to glorify God through all you do. Make a decision to be used only for your intended God given purpose. It's never ok for anyone to be abused, to be used for a purpose not intended. Don't tolerate abuse!

There are many women who are being abused in relationships today. Maybe it's you or someone you know. It took me many years to realize I deserved better. My views were distorted by the pain I had on the inside. My vision was clouded and I was broken.

When I got into this relationship I was already wounded. I was using this relationship like a band aid on a gun shot wound. I was still wounded and hurting on the inside and ran to the pain instead of healing.

The void that I was trying to fill is now being filled with God. Developing an intimate personal relationship with the Father has allowed me to be fulfilled. Paul said in [12]Philippians 4:11 "Not that I speak in respect of want, for I have learned, in whatsoever state I am, therewith to be content." According to [13]U.S. English Thesaurus, being content means to be fulfilled, satisfied or comfortable.

Becoming a true man or woman of God means you will allow God to instruct and direct your life and learn to be fulfilled and satisfied with Him.

If you are in an abusive relationship you have to realize that you deserve better. Please understand that God gave up His best to give you His best, so don't settle for anything less than God's best.

If you have come out of an abusive relationship, I applaud you. I applaud you for your courage and strength to leave. Sometimes it takes more strength to walk away than it does to stay. Don't allow the residue from that past relationship to keep you in bondage or dictate your life now. Let God heal you and make you whole.

WHY DO I ALWAYS CHOOSE THE WRONG MAN?

When I finally got out of the abusive relationship, I was still looking for love in all the wrong places. I spent a few more years in unrewarding and unproductive relationships. I started going to church. I was at a place in my life where I knew I needed the Lord and it was time for me to make a commitment. Shortly after going to church, I attended a singles retreat that changed my life. There was one question on the questionnaire that overwhelmed and frightened me. There were several other questions but that one I will never forget. The question that was asked was, "What do you want in a man?" I was stuck. That's something I had never thought about before. I couldn't answer that question. I had been in a few relationships over the years but didn't know the answer to that question. I never really knew what I wanted in a man or in a relationship. The only answer I could come up with was, "he has to be a man." Pretty sad huh?

After the end of another unproductive relationship, one day, I found myself standing in my bathroom looking in the mirror. I asked myself a question. By this time I was very frustrated and desperate for a change. I found myself saying out loud, "Why do I always choose the wrong man."

After the retreat I realized that the men I had dated were not what I wanted for myself. I settled because I wanted to be in a relationship and that's all I knew. I was still looking for love in all the wrong places and still trying to fill a void.

After asking that question, The Lord spoke to me and said, "That's the problem, **you're choosing**". I then realized at that point that I had been going about this thing all wrong. As I continued to grow in God, I was still very needy, emotionally fragile and didn't understand many things.

A few weeks after the Lord replied to the statement I made in the bathroom, I was out with friends. The topic of conversation just happened to fall on some things I was going through in my life. I remember my best friend told me that I wasn't responsible for anyone except myself and my children. I was shocked. I had spent most of my life feeling responsible for everyone around me. No one had ever told me any different. These words really shook me up. I remember saying "I would give my right arm if I thought it would help someone." When I think about that now, it frightens me. I have given quite a bit in my life but I'm so glad I still have my right arm and I choose to keep it. I've learned to create boundaries in my life. That day I realized I had to make some changes. I realized all the stress and difficulty I was going through was because I was taking on things that didn't belong to me. But I still didn't understand why.

I was determined to know what was going on in my life. As I continued to seek the Lord, He began to reveal that I was co-dependant. I had never even heard this word before.

God reminded me as he began to explain co-dependence to me, that I had spent many years of my life trying to fix my family. At one time I remember thinking, that everyone is addicted to something except me. I always believed that there were no exceptions to the rule. That day I found out that there was really no exception to the rule. Yes everyone was addicted to something and so was I! I couldn't believe I had an addiction too! I didn't drink, smoke or do drugs. What could I possibly be addicted to? My addiction was

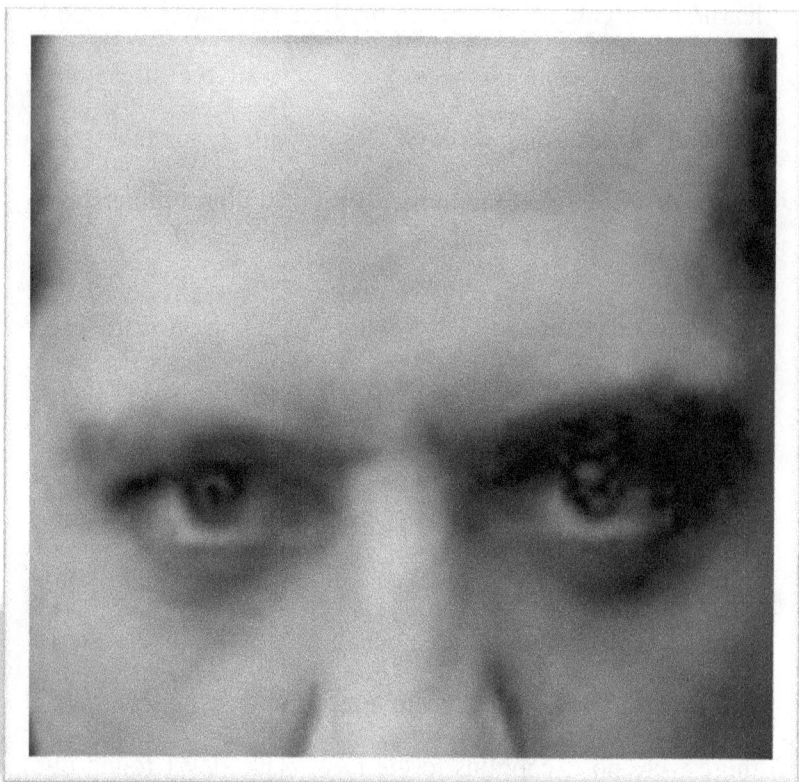

relationships. I had a need to be needed.

The Lord answered my question that day. **I choose these types of men because I have a need to be needed**. So, my drug of choice wasn't cocaine, cigarettes or alcohol. My drug was the needy man instead of the self sufficient man. My choice was always the one I could help.

Codependence is an addiction to people, behaviors or things. In ₁₄Dr. Robert Hemfelt's book, Love is a Choice, He says, "It is the fallacy of trying to control interior feelings by controlling people, things and events on the outside." Dr. Hemfelt list many different characteristics of someone who is co dependant. There are some behaviors I now understand that were obvious in my life during that time; such as low self esteem, thinking that my happiness hinged on others, feeling responsible for others, worried about things I couldn't change, trying to make changes when I could, and looking for something that was lacking or missing in my life.

I had been somebody's "girlfriend" since I was nine years old. I didn't have a clue what I wanted. At the age of nine I should have been developing tasks to develop a sense of accomplishment, ₁₅(education.com) but I was somebody's girlfriend and I was too busy trying to find out what they wanted to even think about what I needed.

I finally understood what the problem was in my life. After all this I realized I wasn't capable of making the right choice when it came to a mate. I didn't have the right information to make an intelligent decision. I spent many years making the wrong choices because I wasn't operating from a position of strength but from a position of needing to be needed.

Knowing what the problem was, I decided to stand still and wait on the Lord.

CHAPTER 6

FOUND BY THE RIGHT MAN

After I realized I had made many bad choices when it came to choosing men, I decided I was not going to date again until I knew God's hand was in my decision. I knew if I put my hand in it, it would only lead to another dead end relationship. I was determined not to make another choice without first consulting the Lord. So, for almost two years I didn't date anyone. I occupied my time getting to know God intimately. I spent lots of time in church, attending Bible study, Sunday school, intercessory prayer, singing in the choir and fellowshipping with the saints of God. This was a very exciting time in my life and I was learning about God and what He required of me.

As I continued to grow in God, I realized my desire to be married was very strong. The enemy was constantly fighting me and reminding me of my singleness. I remember one day hearing the enemy speak to me saying, "You may as well get use to your life the way it is, because you are going to be single the rest of your life." At first I was devastated

33

and I started to cry, but then I got mad with the devil. How dare you contradict the promise of God for my life. I called my best friend and told her I was going to put my wedding dress up. A couple of weeks later I had my wedding dress on hold at a bridal shop. I remember my friend saying to me, "When the clerk at the bridal shop asked you when the wedding date was you gave him the date very confidently, like you were dating". We still laugh about that today.

I purchased my wedding dress when I wasn't dating anyone because after hearing the enemy speak to me I realized I had to step out on faith. This act of faith was my preparation to receive the promise from God. I knew I was going to be married. I didn't know when but, I knew I had to prepare.

I continued to wait on God occupying myself with the things of the Lord. There were many times I felt very isolated and alone. I remember asking the Lord to just let someone say hello to me. At this time no one would even speak to me because God had a hedge around me. I felt invisible.

There was a particular day at work that I recall. I

answered the phone and it was the pharmacy calling to check on the patient's intravenous supplies. As I began to give the young lady the information she needed, she said, "Oh by the way, Jeff said hello." You can probably imagine how excited I was. I almost fell off the chair. Of course, I didn't know he would be my husband at that time. I was just in awe at how God had answered my request for someone to say hello to me. I talked briefly to Jeff and we exchanged phone numbers.

My best friend and I had developed a collection of questions we would ask any perspective men we would talk to. We laugh about that now but, I remember talking to him with this list of questions in my hand, going down the list writing in his answers.

I have learned the time of dating is very crucial, especially for Christians. I don't think it should take a long time to decide if the person you are dating is the one you should marry.

Dating should be a very exciting time. You should have fun together and spend time getting to know each other. The acronym for **D.A.T.E.** the Lord gave me is **Designated**

Authorized Time of Evaluation. I believe there should be a designated amount of time for a person to determine if the person they are dating is the one they should marry. I can't tell anyone what that designated time may be but I encourage you to seek the Lord and listen to what He is saying to you. The time of dating should be used to gather information, to evaluate, to see how they respond to things, how they treat the people around them, to evaluate how they live and to be sensitive to any red flags God may show you.

My husband said he knew I was his wife after our first date. He told me this after we had dated for two weeks. I wasn't convinced because I was determined not to get in God's way. We continued to date and finally I got the memo.

CLEANING HOUSE

We continued to see each other almost everyday until we were married. During our dating time, the Lord showed me in a vision my husband carrying out bags and bags of garbage from my house. I got a little upset and was thinking to myself, "He doesn't know me well enough to be cleaning up my house; he has a lot of nerves." The Lord told me this vision was symbolic of the condition of my heart.

He was using my husband to clean all the junk out of my heart. Even though the Lord had me in preparation for almost two years waiting for my husband, I still had a lot of junk from my past that I had to get over.

When I met my husband he had a three year old and a five year old. My children were thirteen and eighteen. As I said before, I was fifteen when I had my first child and I spent most of my teenage years being a mother. My children were older and very independent. I really had to think if I wanted to take on the task of raising more children.

As we continued to spend time together, I realized I had to make a choice. I didn't feel an obligation to make a choice based on what he wanted but this choice was totally based on what I desired and what I believed God was saying to me. Because I loved him I made the choice to marry him and deal with everything that came along with him, children and all.

This was the first time in my life I had made a conscious decision about a relationship from my heart and spirit and it was very empowering for me.

THE BLENDED FAMILY

We had many turbulent times as we all were blending as a family. Early in the marriage, it seemed like everyone was fighting to find their place in this new family.

For many years before I got married it was only myself, my son and my daughter. My two children had to adjust to the role that this new man played in our lives. They were determined that he wasn't going to take the place of their father. Time has only permitted them to have a relationship that is second to none. He has a special place in his heart for them and so do they. He has shown my thirty three year old son how to be a man and a man of God by example. He has shown my twenty eight year old daughter how a man should treat her and that she is valuable. Over the past fifteen years he has taught them invaluable lessons about life, love and relationships. These were things that needed to come from a positive male role model. He has not replaced their father but he has enhanced and enriched their lives by sacrificing and investing as a father would into them to help them to be God loving and God fearing assets to society.

Just as my two children had to adjust to this new family

so did my husband's two children. They were very young when we came together and it was a lot they didn't understand. God has used me to help rear them and impart into them. My development into a mother to them has not been without resistance. After many years of testing and trials we have persevered. We have stood through the storm. I love them as if they were my own and they have grown to respect and love me unconditionally. I remember recently talking to my youngest daughter; I was saying something about giving birth to four children. She laughed and reminded me that I only birthed two children. I told her I couldn't tell the difference.

A number of couples who come together in a blended family may refer to the children as step children and the parents as steps. My husband has said since the beginning, "There are no steps in this house." After fifteen years we have become blended. We have merged together, with the help of the Lord, into a family that has no "steps". Finally everyone has learned their rightful places and we are very close. We have family meetings, family dinners and have even created a family tradition of spending Christmas Eve together.

After fifteen years of marriage we have learned to love all of our children unconditionally, support them and resolve issues. God has smiled on us as we continue as a family to build His kingdom. I know I made the right choice!

CHAPTER 7

LEARNING TO FORGIVE

As a health care professional, I learned in school that hypertension is called the silent killer because it may have no symptoms at all. It begins to destroy you from the inside out. There could be so much pressure on the blood vessels that a person could be walking around looking healthy one minute and pass out with a stroke the next.

Unforgiveness is similar to hypertension. It too is a silent killer. It destroys you from the inside out. A person could be looking ok on the outside but being eaten away on the inside by the torment of unforgiveness.

A few years ago I started having abdominal pain that wouldn't go away. I was depressed and tired all the time. I stayed at the doctor's office and I had every test you could think of. In February of 2008 I had a surgical procedure done to relieve the pain. The pain came right back. In September of 2008 I had another surgical procedure hoping to relieve the pain but to no avail.

I began to ask God what was going on in my life. He

began to show me how the enemy was using unforgiveness as a poison to destroy me. It was causing me constant sickness in my body. I was broken on the inside and didn't know it. I was emotionally numb, physically tired, mentally drained and just going through the motions to get through the day.

Many people won't even admit to having unforgiveness in their hearts. I think it's important to ask God to show you if there is any unforgiveness in your heart so He can reveal it and remove it.

I spent many years seeking the Lord, trying to figure out what the hindrance was in my life. When the Lord showed me that I had unforgiveness in my heart I was surprised. As I began searching, I realized that there were many people, past and present, that I was holding unforgiveness towards. Let me share with you three of those people and how God dealt with me: The first person was the person who physically abused me for many years. One day I was at work and the Lord asked me if I had forgiven the person that physically abused me. I kind of chuckled inside and said "Yea, I think I have."

That was the first phase of forgiveness for this person in my life. I've spent many years since that time seeking the Lord for closure in this situation.

The second person was my mother. My mother died 22 years ago. We had a great relationship and I loved her dearly. So, you can imagine my surprise when God showed me, just recently, I was holding unforgiveness towards her. During my mothers pregnancy with me I was rejected by her because she was sick. When God revealed this to me I knew He was bringing it to the light to deliver me from the spirit of rejection. I didn't realize I was holding unforgiveness towards my mother.

The third person was my father. At forty five years old I became very angry and feelings of abandonment began to overwhelm me. At first, I didn't know why I was feeling this way but as I begin to seek the Lord, He started to show me. I was feeling abandoned and rejected by my father. I had been carrying these emotions for forty three years, never knowing what was causing them. My biological father died when I was two years old. I never knew him. I don't have a picture of him and I don't know any of his family. Any girl who doesn't have a relationship with her father could have many different issues because of this.

Fathers leave their children for many different reasons. Some reasons are beyond their control and some reasons are within their control, but the effects of growing up without a father are the same. Feelings of abandonment, hurt, rejection, anger or depression may dominate your life for a period of time because of this.

Even though my father died, he still left me and the feelings I had were the same as if he had just walked out. The bottom line is that he wasn't there and I (like many other females) needed him to be there. I was holding unforgiveness towards my father in my heart and I realized I had to let it go.

As God began these processes in my life I had to make a conscious decision to forgive everyone He had shown me I was holding unforgiveness towards. I knew I needed closure.

Maybe your father wasn't in your life either. Maybe he was at one time and now he's not. Maybe you were in an abusive relationship, or maybe you still are. Maybe your mother rejected you. Maybe you were adopted. Maybe the one you needed to love you pushed you away.

Whatever your story is, whoever hurt you, whoever disappointed you, who ever rejected you, you have to forgive them.

As I said everyone has a story to tell. The things you have experienced may be so awful you can't imagine forgiving. I know your life hasn't been a bed of roses but I think it's important to allow God to utilize everything that you have been through for His Glory.

16Ephesians 6:12 says, "For we wrestle not against flesh and blood, but against principalities, against powers, against the rulers of the darkness of this world, against spiritual wickedness in high places."

Please remember that before you were born God had a plan for your life, a good plan. Satan realizes God has something good for your life. He has been trying since the beginning of time to destroy what God loves.

When we get the realization of who we are really fighting against we will be better able to forgive the person. God doesn't love the sin, the abuse, the hurt, or the disappointment, but He loves the sinner. We don't have to ever have a relationship with the person who hurt us but we have to forgive if we want God's plan for our life.

When you continue to walk in unforgiveness you open up the door for the enemy in your life. Unforgiveness is disobedience to God and disobedience to God will bring a curse on your life. [17]Deuteronomy 28:15 says, "But it shall come to pass, if thou wilt not hearken unto the voice of the LORD thy God, to observe to do all his commandments and his statues which I command thee this day; that all these curses shall come upon thee, and overtake thee." [18]Matthew 6:15 says, "But if ye forgive not men their trespasses, neither will your father forgive your trespasses." If you don't forgive, you won't be forgiven by God.

As unforgiveness is a poison, forgiveness is the antidote. Faith is the key but forgiveness unlocks the door. Forgiving someone is never for them, it's always for you. If you have spent many years of your life holding on to unforgiveness, you have to realize that it is destroying your life. You are not experiencing your best life. Unforgiveness could be the culprit behind your sickness. It could be blocking your flow to God. It could be the cause of the inner turmoil you might be experiencing.

I know it's not easy to forgive someone that has hurt you. I had to realize that forgiving is an individual choice each and everyone has to make. When you forgive you don't release the person from the consequences they are going to have to face for what they did to you; by forgiving you release yourself from the torment of continually reliving the pain over and over again. Forgiveness will change your perspective and allow you to walk in the freedom of God.

The Lord told me that every time I pray for the person that abused me, I was releasing myself from the shackles of unforgiveness. It was difficult for me to do this at first but I am daily making the decision to forgive everyone who has ever done anything to hurt me in any way. I am also making a conscious decision to evaluate my heart regularly to make sure nothing is trying to creep back in.

FORGIVENESS
is not something
we do for OTHER PEOPLE.
We do it for OURSELVES
-to GET WELL and
MOVE ON.

CHAPTER 8

BEING MADE WHOLE

I always knew there was something that wasn't right in my life. For many years after giving my life to the Lord, I always felt that there was something blocking me from really moving forward in God. I knew I wasn't ok but I could never figure out what the problem was. I now realize I was fragmented and imprisoned by my past. I spent lots of time crying out to God to help me. I didn't know the first step to take. I didn't know who to ask and I felt hopeless at times. In my desperation, as I continued to seek the Lord, He asked me the same question Jesus asked the man at the pool in [19]John 5:2-9. **"Will you be made whole?"**

I had to really think about this. You might say what kind of question is this? Anyone in their right mind who is struggling with their past should want to be delivered. Who would want to stay in this condition?

As I begin to evaluate where I was, I realized something about myself I had never noticed before. I was comfortable in the place I was in. I was unhappy and miserable but I was comfortable. You may wonder how you could be miserable and comfortable at the same time. I was in a familiar, safe place and it was easy for me to stay like I was. This question really shook me up. It shook me up because I had spent most of my life in this miserable state. This was who I had become. At first glance, (I began to think) I'm really not *that messed up*. I have a good marriage, wonderful children, homes, cars, I'm pastoring a church and I have a good job. What more could I ask for?

I was just like the man at the pool. I had been messed up so long I wasn't ready to let go of who I had become. I had to first get my mind adjusted to the change that was about to occur in my life. I was use to being emotionally impotent. Always making excuses for my condition.

I have always desired to have a place in my home set aside for personal time with God. A few years ago my youngest son moved out and I was able to take his room as my office and prayer room. I began to spend more time with the Lord allowing Him to speak to me and continue to deal with me on being made whole. I wish I could tell you that after the Lord asked me this question I was miraculously transformed and delivered. Unfortunately that wasn't the case.

After much pondering, I decided that I needed the Lord to do this in my life more than I needed anything else. As my mind began to change I was able to trust God to take me through this process of "being made whole". I was hoping that once I said yes I would wake up with everything behind me. The first thing I had to do was learn to put my past in proper perspective and let it go.

LETTING GO OF THE PAST

In some instances, in order for me to let go of my past and get closure, I have had to make a phone call to have a conversation. I have had to write a letter. I have had to sit in front of an empty chair and speak from my heart.

So many people stay in their hurt and pain because they don't want to embrace the process of coming out. Sometimes coming out is just as painful as staying in. I realized I would never become what God created me to be if I didn't embrace this process.

I want to encourage you to move in God's timing in your

journey. Let the Lord lead you out of your past as He desires and on his schedule. As you allow God to take you through this process, you will begin to put your past in the right perspective. If you don't put your past in the right perspective, it will continue to dictate your future. [20]**Perspective is defined as a mental view**. What is your mental view of what has happened to you? Do you understand that God can get some good out of what you have been through? If you can begin to see yourself the way God sees you, you will have a better understanding of the plan of God for your life. As long as you see yourself as the victim you will always fall prey to the enemy's tricks. Your vision will continue to be clouded until you can let go, because it's only holding you back. Whatever might have happened to you in your life, that shouldn't be your focus. Your focus should be on where you are now and where you are going. The enemy wants to keep you focused on that part of your life because he knows if you get freed from it you will find out who you really are. You are not what happened to you. The shame and guilt is not yours. [21]Amos 3:3 says, "Can two walk together, except they be agreed?" You must begin to walk out of agreement with the pain, the shame and the guilt. When you do this over time the hold will be released. Focus on who you really are. God's word says $_{22}$"All things work together for good to them that love God, to them who are the called according to his purpose." Every bad thing, God can work it out for your good. Make your mission to be made whole as you put and keep your past in perspective. Let God use it for good. You know that you have put your past in perspective when you can look back without going back. In other words, you can talk about it and if it happens to come across your mind you don't feel the anger, the hurt or whatever you felt before. When you have forgiven and put your past in perspective, you can think about it or talk about it, and share your testimony with the victory God has given you. You can talk about it, remember it and allow God to use it for His glory. That's when you will know you are not the victim but you are the victor!

Being Made Whole!

CONCLUSION

I always thought the phrase "wounded healer" was defined as someone who brings healing to others while still being broken and wounded themselves, without ever overcoming. I now realize that this is only true when we hide our wounds. It is only when we allow our wounds to be a source of healing to others that we are true wounded healers.

In an article entitled [23]The Wounded Healer by Henri J. Nouwen he states, "Nobody escapes being wounded. We all are wounded people, whether physically, emotionally, mentally, or spiritually. The main question is not 'How can we hide our wounds?' When our wounds cease to be a source of shame, and become a source of healing, we have become wounded healers. Jesus is God's wounded healer: through his wounds we are healed. Jesus' suffering and death brought joy and life. His humiliation brought glory; his rejection brought a community of love. As followers of Jesus we can also allow our wounds to bring healing to others."

This is a portion of my story that the Lord has released

me to share. I share this without shame or embarrassment because I now understand the freedom and liberation in my testimony. This freedom is not just for me but for those who hear it. God did not bring me out and allow me to rise above these things to stay bound.

The wounds of your past should not keep you in bondage. The things that happened in your life should be the vehicle by which you are able to help someone else. If Jesus is our wounded healer and His life's journey was significant, then your journey has not been in vain, no matter how difficult. Allow what you have been through to be an instrument that exposes the enemy. It is only when light comes into the darkness that the darkness leaves. When the light consumes the darkness life can begin. The Bible says [24]"We overcome him by the blood of the Lamb, and the word of our testimony." The hurting and broken are waiting. Ask the Lord to prepare you and give you a platform to share your truth. The path to healing awaits you with open arms. Share your story and be free.

THE WOUNDED SPIRIT

BREAKING FREE FROM THE WOUNDS OF YOUR PAST

REFERENCES

1 The National Health Institute of Mental Health
2 www.epochtime.com
3 www.epochtime.com Article by Thomas Verny
4 www.epochtime.com Article by Dr. Deepak Chopra
5 Nelson King James Version Bible Holy Bible
  Luke 1:41 pg. 1105
6 Comfort for the Wounded Spirit by Frank and
  Ida Mae Hammond page 21
7 www.ChrisFieldBlog.com
8 www.dictionary.com
9 Nelson King James Version Bible Holy Bible
  Romans 8:35 pg. 1230
10 www.eHow.com Effects of Teenage Pregnancy
11 www.relationship-tips-for-you.com
12 Nelson King James Version Bible Holy Bible
  Philippians 4:11 pg. 1281
13 U. S. English Thesaurus
14 Love Is A Choice by Dr. Robert Hemfelt, Dr. Frank Minirth
  and Dr. Paul Meier Pg. 11
15 www.education.com
16 Nelson King James Version Bible Holy Bible
  Ephesians 6:12 pg. 1277
17 Nelson King James Version Bible Holy Bible
  Deuteronomy 28:15 pg. 249
18 Nelson King James Version Bible Holy Bible
  Matthew 6:15 pg. 1043
19 Nelson King James Version Bible Holy Bible
  John 5:2-9 pgs. 1153-1154
20 American Heritage Dictionary
21 Nelson King James Version Bible Holy Bible
  Amos 3:3 page 995
22 Nelson King James Version Bible Holy Bible
  Romans 8:28 page 1230
23 The Wounded Healer Henry Nowden
24 Nelson King James Version Bible Holy Bible
  Revelation 12:11 pg. 1346

THE WOUNDED SPIRIT

Purchase the Two Part

Teaching Series on the Wounded Spirit

&

The Audio Version of this book

by Pastor Regina Holliday

Contact Information:

Pastor Regina Holliday

P.O Box 800

Monee, IL 60449

healingforthewoundedspirit@yahoo.com

www.healingforthewoundedspirit.org

reginaholliday@aol.com

THE WOUNDED SPIRIT

BREAKING FREE FROM THE WOUNDS OF YOUR PAST